My Very First Bible

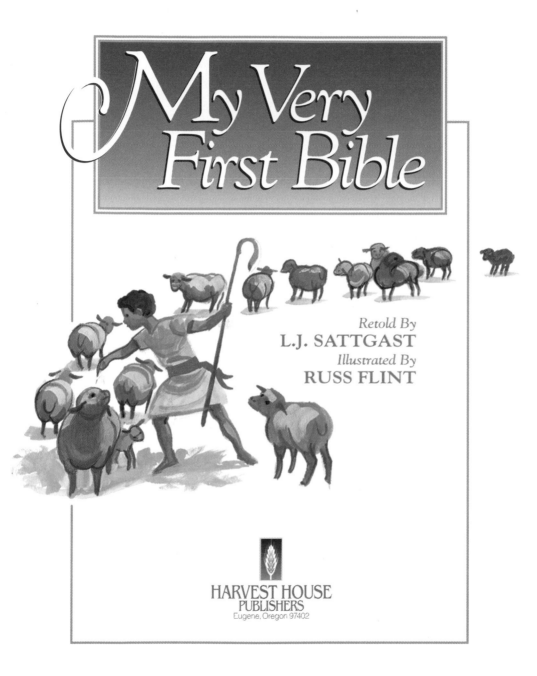

Retold By
L.J. SATTGAST

Illustrated By
RUSS FLINT

HARVEST HOUSE
PUBLISHERS
Eugene, Oregon 97402

For Caleb and Allison

MY VERY FIRST BIBLE

Copyright © 1995 by L.J. Sattgast
Illustration copyright © 1995 by Russ Flint
Published by Harvest House Publishers
Eugene, Oregon 97402

Library of Congress Cataloging - in - Publication Data

Sattgast, L. J., 1953 –
　　　My very first Bible / L.J. Sattgast ; illustrated by Russ Flint.
　　　　　　　p.　　　cm.
　　　Summary: A collection of sixty-one Bible stories.
　　　ISBN 1-56507-352-5
　　　1. Bible stories. English.　　　　[1. Bible stories.]　　　I. Flint, Russ.
　　ill.　　　　II. Title
　　BS551.2.S34　　　　　1995
　　221.9'505–dc20　　　　　　　　　　　　　　　　95- 13304
　　　　　　　　　　　　　　　　　　　　　　　　　　　　　CIP
　　　　　　　　　　　　　　　　　　　　　　　　　　　　　AC

Printed in the United States of America
　　　99　00　01　02 - 10　9　8　7　6　5　4　3　2

Presented to

Teri

From

Grandma

On

I Do not Know

Contents

Old Testament

New Testament

In the Beginning

Genesis 1, 2

A long time ago God made the world.

At first it was dark and empty.

But then God said, "Let there be light!"

The light appeared and God smiled.
Now there was light and dark.
This was the very first day.

On the second
day God made
the sky to sit
above the water.

On the third day God made dry land.
He filled the land with plants and
trees and beautiful flowers.

10

On the fourth day God made the sun.
Then he made the moon and stars that
shine at night.

On the fifth day God made all the animals
that swim in the ocean. And he made all
the birds that fly in the sky.

On the sixth day God made all the
animals that walk and crawl and jump.

13

Then God made a man and a woman.
He called them Adam and Eve, and he
put them in charge of all the animals.

God saw that everything he had
made was very good.
Then God rested on the seventh day.

The Talking Snake

Genesis 3

Adam and Eve lived in a beautiful garden.
"You may eat the fruit from all the trees
in the garden except one," said God.
"If you eat that fruit you will die!"

16

But the crafty snake
came to Eve and said,
"You will not die! If you
eat the fruit, you will be
as wise as God!"

Eve saw how nice the fruit looked.
She took a bite and gave some to Adam.
Then Adam and Eve were afraid because
they had disobeyed.

"Where are you?" called God.

"We were afraid, so we hid," said Adam.

"Did you eat the fruit I told you not to eat?" asked God.

"Eve gave it to me!" said Adam.

"The snake tricked me!" said Eve.

19

God was sad. "Because you disobeyed,"
he said, "you must leave this garden."
Then he sent angels to keep everyone out.

Adam and Eve were sad that they had
disobeyed God. From that time on they
had to work hard for their food.

The Rain and the Rainbow

Genesis 6–9

Adam and Eve had many children.
But they did not obey God.
There was only one man who still
obeyed God. His name was Noah.

"Build a big boat," God told Noah.
"I am going to cover the world with water."
So Noah and his sons built a great big boat.

When the boat was finished,
the animals began to come.

The bears shuffled.
The horses neighed.
And the dogs barked.

But they all went up into
the great big boat.

When Noah and his family and all the animals were safe inside the boat, God shut the door. Then down came the rain and up came the water until it covered the highest mountain.

At last the rain stopped,
and the water went down.
The boat came to rest on
the top of a mountain.

Noah opened a window and sent
out a dove. The dove came back with
an olive branch in its beak.
It was almost time to get out of the boat!

At last God said,
"It is time to come out!"

The goats skipped.
The monkeys chattered.
And the lions stretched as if
to say, "We're glad to be out, too!"

Then God put a rainbow in the sky.
"The rainbow will remind you of
my promise," he said.
"I will never cover the world with
water again!"

A Promise to Abraham

Genesis 12, 15, 18, 21

Abraham and Sarah lived in Haran.
They had lots of goats and sheep
and donkeys, but they had no children.

Then God said, "It is time to move to a
new country. I will show you where to go."
So Abraham and Sarah left Haran.

One night Abraham looked at the stars.
"Try to count the stars," said God.
"That is how big your family will grow."
And Abraham believed what God said.

Many years went by. At last Sarah said,
"I am too old now to have a baby."
But God said, "Is anything too hard for me?"

God did not forget his promise.
A year later Sarah had a baby boy.
Abraham and Sarah called him Isaac.

Sarah was so happy!
"Who would believe that an old woman
like me would have a baby!" she said.

What the Camels Brought

Genesis 24

Abraham called his servant one day.
"Go visit my relatives," he said,
"and find a wife for my son, Isaac."

So the servant started on his way.
Can you count how many camels he took?

At last the servant stopped at a well.
"O Lord," he prayed, "help me find a wife
for Isaac."

Just then a girl named Rebekah came by.
"May I have some water?" asked the servant.
"Yes," said Rebekah, "and I will draw water
for your camels, too!"

The ten camels were happy to get a drink
after their long journey!

The servant stayed with Rebekah's family.
Then he asked her, "Will you marry Isaac?"
What do you think she said?

She said yes! Rebekah left her family's nice house and went to marry Isaac. They lived in a tent and were very happy!

Favorite Sons
Genesis 25, 27

Isaac and Rebekah had twin boys.
Esau was red and hairy, while Jacob
was smooth and fair.

43

When the boys grew up, they were as
different as the sun and the moon.
Esau liked to hunt wild animals, but Jacob
was a quiet man who liked to stay home.

One day Isaac called for Esau and said,
"Go hunting and bring me some tasty meat.
Then I will bless you before I die."

But when Esau left, Rebekah dressed Jacob
in Esau's clothes. "Go get your brother's
blessing," she said.

Isaac was old and could no longer see.
He touched and smelled Jacob. Then he said,
"Here is your blessing, Esau: May God give
you riches, and may everyone else serve you!"

When Esau came back he found out
that he had been tricked. From then
on Esau was angry with Jacob.

God Is with Jacob

Genesis 28, 29

Jacob said goodbye to his family and
started out on a long journey.
He was going to visit his relatives.

One night Jacob dreamed that he saw
a ladder going up to heaven.
He saw angels on it, and he heard God say,
"I will be with you wherever you go!"

In the morning Jacob made a pile of stones.
He poured oil on the stones to show that
he was going to follow God.

After many days, Jacob came to a well
near his uncle's town. "Who is that girl?"
he asked some shepherds.
"It is Rachel, the daughter of Laban,"
they replied.

Jacob liked Rachel as soon as he saw her.
"Your father is my uncle," he told her.
"I have traveled a long way to see him."

Laban had two daughters. Leah was the
oldest, but Rachel was the prettiest.
"I will work for you seven years if you will
let me marry Rachel," said Jacob.
"All right," agreed Laban.

But when it was time
for Jacob to marry,
Laban tricked him and
gave him Leah.

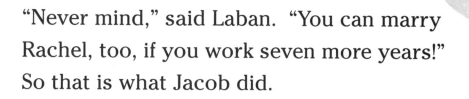

"Never mind," said Laban. "You can marry
Rachel, too, if you work seven more years!"
So that is what Jacob did.

The Bad Brothers

Genesis 37

Jacob had twelve sons,
but he loved Joseph the most.
He even gave him a special coat.

One night Joseph dreamed that his parents
and brothers bowed down to him.

Joseph's brothers didn't like the dream.
"We will never bow down to you!" they said.

The brothers decided to get rid of Joseph.
They took his coat and threw him into a pit.
"Please let me out!" cried Joseph, but his
brothers would not listen.

Then the bad brothers sold Joseph
to some men who came by on camels.
The men took him far away from his
home to the land of Egypt.

Joseph in Prison

Genesis 39, 40

Joseph was sold to a man named Potiphar.
He had to do whatever he was told.

Joseph was a hard worker. So Potiphar put him in charge of his whole house.

But Potiphar's wife lied about Joseph. So Potiphar put him in prison.

Even in prison Joseph worked hard.
One day he saw that two men were sad.
"What is the matter?" Joseph asked.
"We each had a dream," they replied,
"and we don't know what they mean."

Joseph talked with God. Then he told
them the meaning of their dreams.
"One of you will go free tomorrow,"
he said, "but the other will die."
It happened just as Joseph said.

Pharaoh's Dream

Genesis 41

One night King Pharaoh had a dream.
In his dream he saw some cows.

First he saw seven fat cows.

Then seven thin cows came and ate
up the fat cows.
"What does this mean?" asked Pharaoh.

"Joseph can explain dreams," said a servant.

So Joseph was brought to the king.

After he prayed, Joseph explained the dream.

"The seven fat cows mean that there will be seven good years with plenty of food."

"The seven thin cows mean that there will be seven years when food will not grow."

"You must find a wise man to collect
food during the good years," said Joseph.
"Then when the bad years come, there
will be enough to eat."

"Who is wiser than you?" said Pharaoh.
So he put Joseph in charge of the food.

The Brothers Bow Down

Genesis 41– 46

Joseph collected food during the
seven good years.
Then the seven bad years began.
Many people came to Joseph for food.

One day Joseph saw his brothers.
The brothers did not know who he was.
They bowed down and asked for food.

"You must be spies!" said Joseph.

"We are not spies!" said the brothers.

"We have only come to buy food!"

Joseph gave them food, but he put
his silver cup in one of the sacks.
The brothers went on their way,
but soon they saw a servant coming.

"Why did you steal my master's
silver cup?" the servant asked.
The brothers went back to Joseph.
"The one who stole my cup must
be my slave!" said Joseph.
"God is punishing us for what we
did to Joseph," they whispered.

Joseph could not pretend anymore.
He burst into tears and cried, "I am
Joseph, your brother! Don't be afraid.
You did something bad, but God
has turned it into something good!"

Joseph's family came to live in Egypt.
When Jacob saw Joseph he hugged him.
"I never thought I would see you again!"
he said.

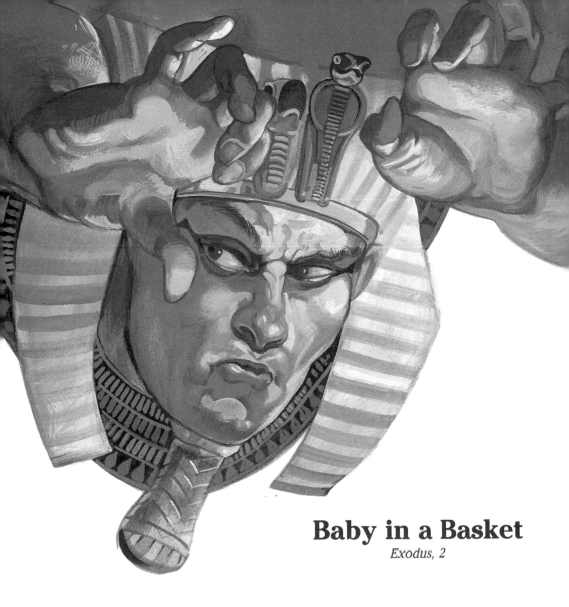

Baby in a Basket

Exodus, 2

A new Pharaoh became king.
He did not like God's people, so he
made this rule: Every new baby boy
must be thrown into the river.

One mother loved her little baby boy. What should she do? At first she tried to hide him.

But that did not work very well.

So she made a basket and covered it with pitch.

76

She put her baby in the basket and let
it float on the river.
The baby's sister hid nearby to see
what would happen.

Pharaoh's daughter came to take a bath.
She saw the basket and looked inside.

"Waah! Waah!"
cried the baby.
"I want to keep
this baby!" said
the princess.

"Shall I find someone to nurse him
for you?" asked the sister.
"Yes!" replied the princess.
The sister ran to get their mother!

His mother took care of him until he could go to the palace.
And the princess called him Moses.

The Burning Bush

Exodus 2–4

When Moses grew up he tried to help
his people. But Pharaoh got mad.
So Moses ran away into the desert.

81

Moses was a shepherd in the desert.
Many years went by, and Moses grew old.
Then one day he saw a bush that was
burning with fire, but it did not burn up.

God talked to Moses
from the bush.
"Go back to Egypt,"
he said, "and take my
people away from there."

But Moses was afraid.

"What if they won't listen?" he said.

"Throw down your staff," said God.

So Moses threw it on the ground.

The staff turned into a snake!
Moses was afraid and ran away.
"Now pick up the snake," said God.
What do you think happened?

The snake turned back into a staff!
"Show the people this miracle if
they won't believe you," said God.

Ten Terrible Plagues

Exodus 5–12

Moses went to Egypt.

"Let God's people go!" he said.

But Pharaoh said, "No!"

After that Pharaoh made the
people work even harder.
"You are lazy!" he said.
The people cried out to Moses.

"What shall we do?" prayed Moses.
"I will send ten terrible plagues," said God.
"After that Pharaoh will let my people go."

First God turned the river water into blood.
Then he sent a plague of frogs. But Pharaoh
still did not listen.

Then God sent
gnats to bite
and sting the
people.

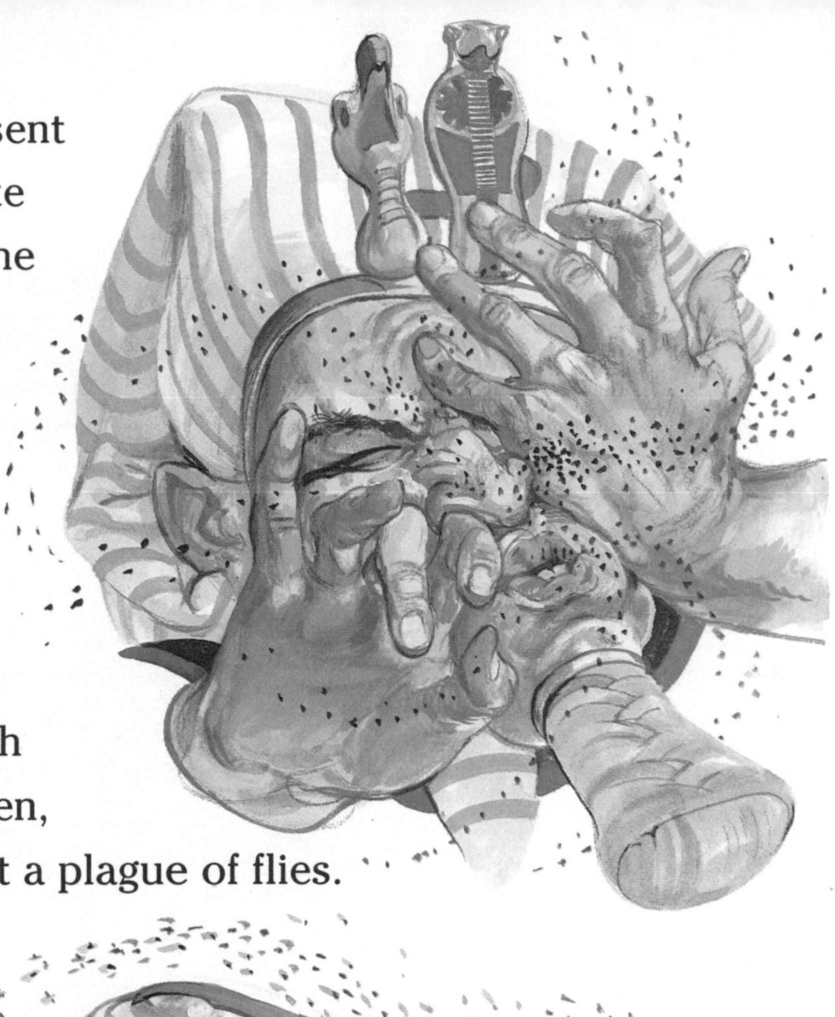

But Pharaoh
did not listen,
so God sent a plague of flies.

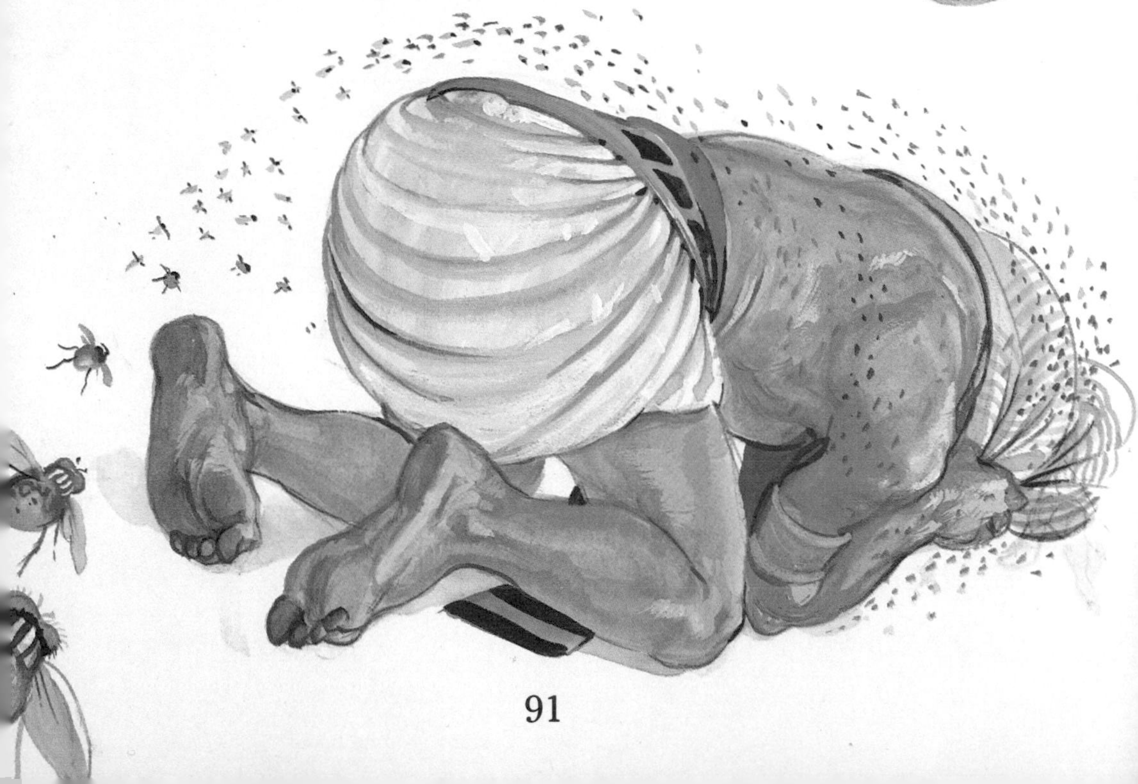

Then God sent a plague on the animals.
They began to get sick and die.
Did Pharaoh obey God then? No, he did not!

So God sent a plague of sores.
And then he sent a plague of hail.
Pharaoh did not like it at all.

God sent a plague of locusts to eat up
the grass and leaves.
Then God made the day turn black as night.
Pharaoh called Moses.
"Don't ever come to see me again!" he said.

"I will send one more plague,"
said God. "So listen and do what I say!"
The people did what God said.
They put the blood of a lamb over their
doors, and they ate a special dinner.

That night all the oldest sons in Egypt died.
But all of God's people were safe.
Pharaoh sent for Moses.
"Go away," he said, "and take
all the people with you!"

The Great Chase

Exodus 12–15

The people of God left Egypt.
God led them by a pillar of cloud during
the day and a pillar of fire at night.

Then Pharaoh changed his mind.
"Bring the people back!" he told
his soldiers.

The people were camped by the sea.
When they saw the soldiers coming,
they were afraid.

But God made a path through the sea.
The people ran across to the other side!

When the Egyptians tried to follow,
the water covered them up.
"God has saved us!" cried the people.

The Ten Commandments

Exodus 19, 20

The people camped in the desert.
Then God came down from heaven
to the top of a mountain.
Moses went up to talk with God.

This is what God said:

Don't worship
anyone but God.

Never bow down
to idols.

Never say God's
name in a bad way.

Remember to rest
on the Lord's day.

Obey your father
and your mother.

Don't get angry
and kill someone.

Love your own wife
or husband and not
someone else's.

Don't steal things
from other people.

Don't tell lies.

Don't wish
for someone
else's things.

The Walls Fall Down

Joshua 1, 6

Joshua was the new leader of Israel.

He led the people to Jericho.
The wall around Jericho was
tall and strong.
How would the people get in?

God told the
people to march
around Jericho
once every day
for six days.
So that is what
they did.

On the seventh day the people marched
around Jericho seven times.
Then the priests blew their trumpets,
the people SHOUTED, and the wall fell down!

The Strongest Man
Judges 13–16

Samson was the strongest man in Israel.

God had told him never to cut his hair.

Samson liked a
pretty woman
named Delilah.
But Delilah was
a Philistine, an
enemy of Israel.

"Please help us," said the Philistines.
"Find out why Samson is so strong."

Day after day Delilah asked Samson
why he was so strong. At last he said,
"If I cut my hair, I will not be strong."

So the Philistines
cut Samson's hair
while he was asleep.

Samson was not strong anymore.
The Philistines took out his eyes.
They made him work hard grinding grain.

One day the Philistines had a party.
They looked at Samson and laughed.
But Samson's hair had grown long again.

He pushed on two of the pillars.
Down came the house with a crash!
Samson and all the Philistines died.

Ruth Finds a Home
Book of Ruth

Naomi was going back to Israel.

Orpah kissed her and left.

But Ruth said, "I will go with you!"

When Naomi reached her home,
her friends were happy to see her.
"Who came with you?" they asked.
"This is Ruth," Naomi replied.

Ruth wanted to help Naomi.
She went to the fields to gather grain
so that they could eat.

Boaz was the owner of the field.
"Make sure you leave plenty of
grain for her," he told his workers.

Naomi was pleased with the grain.
"Go ask Boaz to marry you," she said.
So that is what Ruth did.
Boaz was happy to marry Ruth!
After awhile they had a little boy.

Naomi liked being a grandmother.
"God has made me very happy!"
she said.

A Boy Listens
1 Samuel 1–3

Hannah lived in a good home and
she had a fine husband. But she was
sad because she had no children.

Hannah asked God to give her a son.
"If you will give me a son," she said,
"I will let him serve you."
God answered Hannah's prayer.
She had a baby boy, and she named
him Samuel.

When Samuel was old enough,
Hannah took him to live in
God's house with Eli the priest.

One night someone called Samuel.
He ran to Eli and said, "Here I am!"
But Eli said, "I did not call you."
"Samuel! Samuel!" said the voice again.
At last Eli said, "God is calling you!"

Samuel heard the voice again.
He said, "Speak, Lord. I'm listening!"
Then God talked with Samuel.

Samuel grew up to be a man of God.
He always listened to God, even when
he grew old.

The Shepherd
1 Samuel 17; Psalm 23

David was a shepherd.
All day long he took care of big
woolly sheep and frisky little lambs.
He helped them find grass to eat.

128

He took them to quiet streams where
they could have a drink of water.

Sometimes, David used his sling to scare away hungry lions and bears!

At night, while the sheep slept,
David often sang songs about God.
"God is my Shepherd," he sang.
"He will always take care of me."

A Boy and a Giant
1 Samuel 17

Goliath was big. Goliath was strong.

"Come and fight me!" he shouted.

But the people were afraid of Goliath.

One day David came to the camp.
He was bringing food for his brothers.
David heard what Goliath said.

"I will fight Goliath!" David said.
"How can a young boy fight a giant?"
asked the king.
"God will be with me!" David replied.

The king put his armor on David, but the
armor did not fit, so David took it off.
Then David went down to the stream.
He picked up five smooth stones and
put them in his pouch.

When Goliath saw David, he was angry.
"Why you're just a boy!" he roared.
"You trust in your sword and spear,"
said David, "but I trust in the living God!"

137

David put a stone in his sling and threw
it at Goliath. It hit him on the forehead.
Down crashed Goliath to the ground!

When David grew older, he became king.
The leaders poured oil on his head, and
the people shouted, "Long live the king!"

139

Solomon's Request

1 Kings 3–8

Solomon was David's son. One night,
after he became king, he had a dream.
"Ask me for anything you want,"
God said, "and I will give it to you."

"I want to be a wise king," said Solomon.
God was pleased. He did what Solomon
asked, and he also made him very rich.

Solomon built a beautiful temple so that
people could come and worship God.
Then all the people came to see it.
Solomon prayed, "Watch over us, O Lord,
and listen to us when we pray!"

Fire and Rain

1 Kings 16–18

Ahab worshiped idols instead of God.

"God is not happy with you," said Elijah.

"He is going to stop the rain for a long time.

Ahab did not like what Elijah said.
He wanted to hurt Elijah.
So Elijah hid by a river.
There was nothing to eat there, but God
sent ravens with food to feed Elijah.

When the water in the river dried up, Elijah went to live with a poor widow. The widow and her son shared their food with him. God always gave them enough to eat.

For three years there was no rain.
The land grew drier and dustier.
Then Elijah went to see King Ahab.

"Let's find out if your idols are stronger
than God!" he said.

Ahab's men built an altar and prayed
to their idols. But nothing happened.
"Maybe they are sleeping!" said Elijah.

Then Elijah prayed.
"O Lord, let everyone
know that you are God!"

So God sent fire down from heaven.
It burned up the altar, and all the people
cried, "The Lord, he is God!"

Then Elijah prayed for rain.
At first nothing happened.
But then he saw a small cloud.

The cloud grew bigger and blacker.
Then down came the rain.
How glad the people were to see it!

Josiah Obeys

2 Kings 22, 23

Josiah became king when he was a boy.

When Josiah grew up he noticed
that the temple needed to be fixed.
So he called in the workers.

The workers
found something
in the temple.
It was the Bible!

"Read it to me," said King Josiah.
So someone read the Bible to the king.

Then Josiah called the people together.
They listened as someone read the Bible.
"We will obey God's Word," they said.

The Lion's Den
Daniel 6

Daniel was a very wise man, so the king put him in charge of all the leaders.

155

One day the king
made a rule:
For thirty days you
must only pray to me.
If you don't, I will feed
you to the lions!

The leaders came to the king and said,
"Daniel does not obey your rule.
He prays three times a day to God."

The king was sad, but he could not
break his own rule.
"May your God help you!" he said.
Then they threw Daniel in the lion's den.

Early the next morning, the king ran to the lion's den.

"Daniel," he called, "are you all right?"

"Yes!" answered Daniel.
"God took care of me. He sent an angel
to shut the mouths of the lions!"

The Daring Queen
Book of Esther

The king needed a queen.

He looked at many beautiful women.

"I choose Esther!" he said.

Mordecai had taken care of Esther
from the time she was a little girl.
"Do not tell anyone you are a Jew from
the land of Israel," said Mordecai.

A man named Haman hated Mordecai.
He knew that Mordecai was a Jew, so
he asked the king to make a rule:
All the Jews must die!

Mordecai went to see Queen Esther.
"Go ask the king to save us!" he said.
Esther knew that she was not allowed
to see the king unless he called her.
But she said, "All right, I will go."

The king was pleased to see Esther.
"What do you want?" he asked.

"Come to eat a special dinner with me,"
she replied, "and bring Haman with you."

While they were eating the king said,
"Tell me what you want, Esther."
"Save us from wicked Haman!" she cried.

The king was angry with Haman.
He made a rule to save the Jews.
And he made Mordecai a leader
instead of Haman.

Jonah Runs

Book of Jonah

"Go to Nineveh," God told Jonah.
But Jonah did not want to go. So he
got on a boat and went the other way.

Then God sent a great storm.
"It's my fault," said Jonah. "Throw me
into the water and the storm will stop."

When the men threw Jonah out,
the storm stopped.
Then God sent a great fish to
swallow Jonah.

Jonah was inside the fish three days.
Then he prayed and God heard him.
The fish threw Jonah up onto the land.

"Go to Nineveh," God said again.
And this time Jonah obeyed.

He told the people about God.
The people were sorry for their sins.
"We will obey God," they said.

Going Home
Book of Ezra

God's people got a letter from the king.
The letter said that they could go back to the
land of Israel. Many of the people went back.

When they reached Israel, the people
built a new city and a new temple.
Then they cried and sang for joy.
"God has brought us home!" they said.

New Testament
Stories

A New Baby

Matthew 1; Luke 1, 2

In a little town called Nazareth
there lived a young woman.
Her name was Mary.

One day God sent
an angel to Mary.
At first, Mary was afraid.

But the angel said, "Don't be afraid!
God has chosen you to be the
mother of his Son, Jesus."
"I am happy to do what God wants,"
replied Mary.

Nearby there lived a man named Joseph.
He would soon become Mary's husband.
Joseph was a carpenter. He used his
tools to make things out of wood.

One night Joseph had a dream.
"Mary will have a baby," said an angel.
You must call his name Jesus, for he
will save people from their sins."

Joseph and Mary traveled
to the town of Bethlehem.
It was almost time for
Mary to have her baby.

How tired they were when they
reached that crowded little town!

There was no place
for them to stay
except in a stable
filled with animals.

That night, little baby Jesus was born.
Mary wrapped him in a warm cloth
and laid him in a manger.

In a field nearby, some shepherds were
taking care of their sheep.
It was a peaceful night, and all was quiet.

Suddenly, a bright angel appeared.
At first the shepherds were afraid.
But the angel said, "I have good news!
A baby was born today. He is God's Son.
You can find him in Bethlehem."
Then many angels sang praises to God.

The shepherds hurried to look for Jesus.
How happy they were when they found him!

Where Is the King?

Matthew 2

One night some wise men saw a bright
new star. "Let's follow it," they said.
"It will lead us to a great King!"

The wise men traveled for many days.
When they came to Jerusalem, they asked
King Herod where to find the new baby King.

King Herod did
not know where
to find the baby.
So he asked the
teachers about it.

They looked in the Bible and said,
"A King will be born in Bethlehem."

So the wise men followed the star to Bethlehem.

The star stopped at Joseph and Mary's house. When the wise men saw Jesus, they bowed down and gave him wonderful gifts.

The Missing Boy

Luke 2

Every year Jesus and his family went to Jerusalem to celebrate the Feast of Passover.

Passover was a wonderful holiday.
Jesus would eat a special meal,
and he would hear stories about how
God had helped his people.

Jesus especially loved to visit
the temple in Jerusalem.
It was a place to worship God.

When it was time to go home,
Mary and Joseph started on their way.
But where was Jesus?

Back they went to look for him.
They finally found him in the temple.
He was talking with the teachers.

"We were so worried!" said Mary.
"Didn't you know that I would be here
in my Father's house?" asked Jesus.
He knew that God was his Father.

So Jesus went home with Mary and Joseph.
And he always obeyed them.

Jesus and the Dove

Matthew 3

When Jesus grew up, he went to visit John.

John was talking with the people.

"Stop doing what is wrong!" he said.

The people were sorry for their sins.
"We want to follow God," they said.
So one by one they came to be baptized.

"I want to be baptized, too," said Jesus.
"But you have never sinned," said John.
Jesus replied, "I want to do what is right."

So John baptized Jesus.
God's Spirit came down on Jesus
like a dove. And God said,
"You are my Son, and I love you!"

A Happy Wedding

John 2

One day Jesus and his
friends were invited to
a wedding.
Jesus' mother went, too.
But after awhile, there
was nothing left to drink.

Mary knew that Jesus could help.
So she called the sevants and said,
"Do whatever Jesus tells you to do!"

There were six empty jars nearby.
"Fill them with water," said Jesus.
So the servants obeyed.

Then the servants
took the water and
filled up the glasses.

But it was not water anymore.
Jesus had turned the water into wine!
This showed that Jesus was God's Son.

Twelve Disciples
Luke 6

Jesus had many friends called disciples.
They followed him from town to town.
And they believed what he said about God.

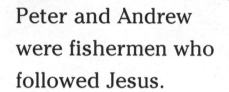

Peter and Andrew
were fishermen who
followed Jesus.

Mary Magdalene
had been sick, but
Jesus made her well.

Matthew collected tax
money from people.
But he left his money
and followed Jesus.

Jesus often stayed
in the home of Mary
and Martha and their
brother Lazarus.

But now Jesus was going to choose twelve disciples to be his special friends. They would stay together, and he would teach them many things.

Jesus went up into the hills to pray.
He asked God to help him choose the
right men to be his special friends.

These are the disciples that Jesus picked:

Peter
1

James
2

Philip
5

Bartholomew
6

Another
James
9

Thaddaeus
10

Can you count them?

John
3

Andrew
4

Matthew
7

Thomas
8

Simon
11

Judas
Iscariot
12

What Jesus Said

Matthew 5–7

Look at all the people!

Can you find Jesus?

He is sitting on the hill.

Listen to what he is saying:

212

You are like a lamp
when you are good.
People can see that
you love God.

God gives sunshine
and rain to everyone.
We should be kind
to everyone, too.

God takes care of
the flowers. He will
take care of you, too.

God hears you
when you pray.

If you obey God, you will be wise like
the man who built his house on a rock.

But if you do not obey God, you will
be like the foolish man. His house fell down
because it was built upon the sand.

A Man Walks

Mark 2

Once there was a man
who could not walk.
His friends had to take
care of him.

One day Jesus came to town.
"Jesus can help!" said the friends.
So they carried the man to see Jesus.
But they could not get in the door.

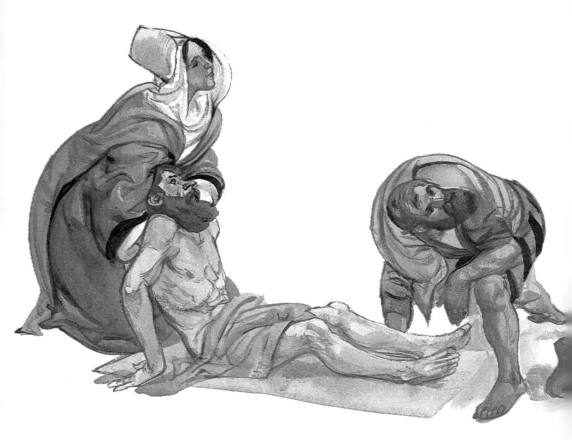

That did not
stop the friends.
They made a hole
in the roof, and they
let the man down
in front of Jesus.

Jesus looked at the man.
"Get up and walk," he said.
The man jumped up.

Everyone began to praise God!
That made the teachers angry. They did
not believe that Jesus was God's Son.

The Wind Obeys

Mark 4

Jesus was tired.
He got into a boat
with his disciples.
Then he lay down,
and soon he was
fast asleep.

Suddenly, a
storm came up.
The disciples were
afraid. "Help us,
Jesus!" they cried.

Jesus got up
and spoke to
the storm.
"Be quiet!"
he said.

The wind stopped
and the water was still.
"Why were you so
afraid?" asked Jesus.
"Why didn't you
trust in God?"
Then the disciples
knew that Jesus
was God's Son.

A Sick Girl

Mark 5

A man named Jairus had one daughter. He loved her very much.

One day his girl got very sick.
Jairus ran to look for Jesus.

When Jairus found Jesus, he begged
him to come to his house.
"You can make my daughter well," he said.
So Jesus went with Jairus.

Just then some men came to Jairus.
"Your little girl has died," they told him.
"So don't bother Jesus anymore."
But Jesus said, "Don't be afraid!"
And on he went to Jairus' house.

When they reached the house,
Jesus took the girl by the hand.
"Little girl," he said, "get up!"
The girl got up. Jesus made her well!

A Bagful of Seeds

Matthew 13

One day, Jesus told this story:

A farmer went out with a bag of seeds.
He tossed the seeds here and there.

Some seeds were
eaten by the birds

Some fell on rocks
and did not grow.

Some seeds fell
among the weeds.

Some fell on good ground
and grew into plants.

We are like the good ground when we
listen to God's Word and obey it.

The Little Boy's Lunch
John 6

Jesus and the disciples were tired.
So they sailed away to find a quiet
place to rest.

But when they landed,
crowds of people came.
Jesus felt sorry for them.
He made many people well.

Soon it was dinner time.

"Give these people some food," said Jesus.

But Philip said, "Where can we find food?"

Andrew found a boy with a small lunch.
"I will give my lunch to Jesus," said the boy.

Jesus blessed the food
and broke it into pieces.

The disciples passed around the food.
Everyone had plenty to eat!

Can you count how many baskets
were left over?

Peter Gets Wet

Matthew 14

One night Jesus wanted to pray.

So he told his disciples to sail on home.

235

In the middle of the night Jesus
walked across the water to the boat.
The disciples were afraid. But Jesus
said, "Don't be afraid. It's just me."

Peter said, "If it's you, tell me to walk on the water." So Jesus said, "Go ahead."

Peter did fine
until he looked
at the waves.
"Help me, Jesus!"
he cried.

Jesus reached out and took his hand.
"Remember to keep your eyes on me," he said.

The Kind Man
Luke 10

A man once asked Jesus a question.

"How do I know when to be kind?"

Then Jesus told this story:

A certain man was beaten and robbed.

"Help me!" said the man when a priest came along. But the priest walked on by.

Soon a Levite came along. Did he help?
No, he hurried past the poor man.

Finally, a Samaritan came by.
He stopped to help the poor man.

The Samaritan put bandages on his
cuts and let him ride on his donkey.

Then he took the poor man to a place
where he could stay and get well.

Jesus finished his story and said,
"Be as kind as the Samaritan."

A Thankful Man

Luke 17

Ten sick men walked down the road.

Everyone ran away from them.

People were afraid of their disease.

The sick men were sad and lonely.

One day they saw Jesus.
Jesus did not run away.
He made them well again.

The ten men were so happy!
Away they ran down the road.

But one man came
back to Jesus.
"Thank you!" he said.

"I healed ten men," said Jesus. "But you
are the only one who said thank you!"

Lost and Found

Luke 15

The teachers did not like Jesus.
"He eats with bad people!" they said.
So Jesus told three stories to show
how much God loves sinners.

Here is the first story:

A shepherd counted
his one hundred sheep.
Uh-oh! One was missing!

The shepherd looked
for his lost lamb.
At last he found him.

He called his
friends to come
and be happy
with him.

God is like a shepherd. He is happy
when one person is sorry for disobeying.

Here is the second story:

A woman had
ten coins. But
one was missing!

She looked and
looked for the
lost coin.

At last she found it.
"Hooray!" she said.

God is glad when one lost sinner is sorry.

Here is the third story:

A man had two sons, but
one of them left home.

The young man spent all his money.
He was hungry, but no one would help him.
So he got a job feeding pigs.

The young man decided to go home.
There was his father watching for him!

His father hugged and kissed him.

"We will have a party for you!" he said.

But the other son was angry.
"I stayed home, and no one gave me a party!"

His father said, "Don't be angry.
We should all be happy because your
brother was lost, but now he is found!"

Jesus Loves Children

Mark 10

One day some children came to see Jesus.
But the disciples said, "Don't bother Jesus!"

Jesus said, "Leave them alone!
Let the children come to me!
Don't you know that God loves children?"

Then Jesus took the children in his arms.
He hugged them and blessed them.

Jesus Helps a Friend
John 11

A messenger came running to Jesus.
"Come quickly!" he said.
"Your friend Lazarus is very sick.
His sisters, Mary and Martha,
want you to come."

Jesus went to see Lazarus.
But Lazarus was already dead.
Mary and Martha were very sad.

Jesus was sad, too.
"Take me to the tomb," he said.

The tomb was a cave.
It had a stone in front.
"Take away the stone!"
commanded Jesus.

Then he said, "Lazarus, come out!"
Out came Lazarus wrapped
in strips of cloth!

Jesus made this promise: "Anyone who
believes in me will live forever!"

Little Man in a Tree
Luke 19

Zacchaeus was short.
His hands didn't quite
reach the shelf.

And his feet didn't
quite reach the floor.

Guess which one is Zacchaeus!

Zacchaeus was a tax collecter.
But he cheated and charged
people too much money.

One day Jesus came to town.
But Zacchaeus was too short to see him
over the crowd.

So he ran to a tree and climbed up.
"Now I can see Jesus!" he thought.

Jesus came by and looked up.
"Come down, Zacchaeus!" he said.
"I am going to your house today!"

Down came Zacchaeus as fast as can be.

"From now on I will not cheat," he said.
"And I will pay back more than I took."
"God has changed your heart!" said Jesus.

Jesus Rides a Donkey

Luke 19

Jesus rode a donkey when
he came to Jerusalem.
"Jesus is our King!"
cried the people.

They waved branches and
shouted, "Hosanna! Hosanna!"

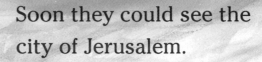

Soon they could see the
city of Jerusalem.

Everyone else was happy, but Jesus was sad. "I wish the people of Jerusalem would listen to me," he said.

When Jesus came to the temple,
he saw people buying and selling.

Jesus drove them out with a whip.
"God's house is not a place to buy and
sell," he said. "It is a place to pray!"

The Last Meal

John 13

It was time for Passover.
So Jesus and his disciples
went to Jerusalem.

274

Before they ate, Jesus washed their dirty feet.
At first Peter said, "No, Jesus!"
But Jesus said, "I am teaching you to help
one another."

As they ate Jesus said, "One of you will hand me over to men who want to kill me. And some of you will run away and leave me."

Then Judas got up and left the room.
But Peter said, "I will never leave you."
"Yes, you will, Peter," Jesus said. "When the
rooster crows you will know that I was right."

The Garden

Matthew 26

After eating, Jesus and his disciples went
to a quiet garden called Gethsemane.
"Come pray with me," said Jesus.

Jesus began to pray.
How sad he was!
He knew what was
going to happen soon.

Jesus looked at his disciples.
He found them fast asleep.
"Why didn't you pray?" he asked.

But now it was too late.

An angry crowd of men was coming.

And Judas was leading the way.

Judas came up to Jesus and kissed him.
Then the men knew which one to grab.
All the disciples ran away, but Peter followed
a little way behind.

The men took Jesus
to the leaders.
"Are you God's Son?"
they asked.
"Yes, I am," said Jesus.
This made the leaders angry.

Peter was waiting outside.

"Are you Jesus' friend?" someone asked.

"No!" said Peter. "I don't even know him!"

Peter heard a
rooster crow.
He remembered
what Jesus had
told him, and he
ran away crying.

285

The Sad Day
Mark 15; John 19

The leaders took Jesus to see Pilate.

Pilate was the governor.

"Are you really a king?" he asked.

"Yes, I am," replied Jesus.

"This man has done
nothing wrong," said Pilate.
But the leaders shouted,
"He must die!"

At last Pilate agreed to do as the leaders wished.

The soldiers took him away.
They made him carry a heavy cross,
and they went to the top of a hill.

There on the cross, Jesus died.
His friends watched from far away.

When Jesus was dead, his friends took
him down from the cross.
They wrapped him in a clean cloth
and put him in a tomb.
It was the saddest day that ever happened.

The Happy Day

Matthew 28; John 20

Early Sunday morning something happened.
The ground shook and an angel appeared.
Quick as a flash he rolled away the stone.
Was Jesus inside? No, he wasn't!

Mary Magdalene came to visit
the tomb, but it was empty.
She ran to tell Peter and John.
Where could Jesus be?

Peter and John left, but Mary stayed
near the tomb. She was crying.
Suddenly, she saw two angels.
"Why are you crying?" they asked.
"Because someone took Jesus away,"
she sobbed.

Then Mary saw a man.
"Did you take him?"
she asked.
"Mary!" said the man.
Then Mary knew who
he was.

It was Jesus! He was alive!
"Go tell my friends that you have
seen me," said Jesus.

That night the disciples were together.
Suddenly, Jesus appeared in the room!
He really *was* alive! What a happy day!

Jesus Says Goodbye
John 21; Acts 1

One night the disciples went fishing.

But they did not catch any fish.

In the morning, they saw Jesus on the shore.

"Throw your nets in again," said Jesus.
This time the net was filled with fish!
Then Jesus ate and talked with them.

Soon after, Jesus took the
disciples up on a hill.
"You must go tell everyone
the good news that I am alive,"
said Jesus.

Then Jesus began to
go up in the air.
Up, up, up he went
until they could not
see him anymore!

Suddenly, they saw two men.
"Don't worry," said the men.
"Jesus will come back someday!"

The New Helper

Acts 2

The disciples were praying together.
Suddenly, they heard a roaring wind,
and they saw flames of fire.
God's Helper, the Holy Spirit, had come!

Other people heard
the noise, too.
"What is happening?"
they asked.

Peter stood up and began to talk.
"God made Jesus alive again," he said.
"And he has sent us his Holy Spirit."

Many people believed in Jesus that day.
First they were baptized.
Then they met together to share their
food and to learn more about God.
They were happy to be in God's family!

The Bright Light

Acts 9

There was one man who hated Jesus.

His name was Saul.

He tried to hurt God's people.

309

Saul was on his way to Damascus. Suddenly, a bright light flashed from the sky. Saul fell to the ground.

Saul heard a voice. It was Jesus!
"Stop hurting my people," said Jesus.
"Now you must tell people about me."

When Saul got up,
he could not see.
He was blind!

But God sent a man to help Saul.
"Jesus has made you well," said the man.

How happy Saul was to see again!
He began to tell everyone about Jesus.
This made some people angry.
But many others believed in Jesus.

Peter Prays

Acts 9

Dorcas was a kind woman.

She made clothes for poor people.

The people all loved Dorcas.
But one day Dorcas got sick.
She did not get well, and
soon she died.

The people were sad.
They ran to find Peter.
"Please come at
once!" they begged.

When Peter came
they showed him the
clothes that Dorcas
had made for them.

Peter prayed and said, "Dorcas, get up!"

Dorcas opened her eyes and sat up.
How happy everyone was!

Peter and the Angel
Acts 12

Peter told people about Jesus.

So King Herod put him in prison.

God sent an angel to the prison.

"Wake up!" he said. "Follow me!"

The angel took Peter out into the city.

Peter went to a friend's house and knocked on the door.

His friends could hardly believe their eyes! "God has answered our prayers!" they said happily.

A Long Journey

Acts 13, 14

Paul and Barnabas said goodbye.

They wanted to start new churches.

So they sailed to other countries.
Then they walked from town to town
telling people they met about Jesus.

Some people did not want to listen.
They chased Paul and Barnabas away.

But others were happy to hear that God
loved them and had sent his Son, Jesus.
More and more people believed in Jesus,
and many new churches were started.

The Shipwreck
Acts 27, 28

Paul was in prison. He was on a ship
that was going to Rome.

Suddenly, a terrible storm began.
"We will all die!" cried the men.
But Paul said, "No one will die!"

Paul was right.
The ship sank,
but everyone
made it to shore.

Paul was in prison many years.
He told all his visitors about Jesus.

Paul wrote letters to his
friends in the churches.
At the end he would say,
"May God be with you!"

Heaven Is
Our Home

Revelation 21, 22
Isaiah 11

Someday Jesus will come back.

He will take everyone who loves
and believes in him to heaven.
Heaven will be a happy place.
No one will cry, and no one will
ever get hurt or die.

Heaven will be a bright place to live.
There won't be any more night.
It will always be day because God will
be there, shining like the sun.

There won't be any fighting in heaven.
All the animals and the children will
play together happily!

Jesus says, "I am coming soon."
And we answer, "Yes, Jesus, please
come soon!"